PRINCIPLES OF
DANCE AND MOVEMENT
NOTATION

Other books by Rudolf Laban

MODERN EDUCATIONAL DANCE
EFFORT *(with F. C. Lawrence, M.C.)*
THE MASTERY OF MOVEMENT
CHOREUTICS

LABAN'S PRINCIPLES OF DANCE AND MOVEMENT NOTATION

by
RUDOLF LABAN

SECOND EDITION
Annotated and edited by
RODERYK LANGE

WITH 114 BASIC MOVEMENT GRAPHS
AND THEIR EXPLANATION

ART WORK BY DIANA BADDELEY

Publishers   PLAYS, INC.   Boston

©

MACDONALD AND EVANS LIMITED
1956, 1975

American edition published by Plays, Inc.
1975

Library of Congress Cataloging in Publication Data

Laban, Rudolf von, 1879–1958.
  Laban's principles of dance and movement notation. *Second edition, revised and annotated by Roderyk Lange.* 1st London ed. (Macdonald & Evans) published in 1956 under title: Principles of dance and movement notation.
  Includes indexes.
  1. Dance notation. 2. Movement notation. I. Title II. Title: Principles of dance and movement notation.

GV1587.L26 1975   793.3′2   75–11503
ISBN 0–8238–0187–X

Filmset by Northampton Phototypesetters Ltd.
Printed in Great Britain by
J. W. Arrowsmith Ltd.
Bristol

FOREWORD

FOR many years Macdonald and Evans have devoted themselves to promoting the work of Rudolf Laban. This second edition of *Principles of Dance and Movement Notation*, prepared with their usual care and understanding, reaffirms the enduring worth of Laban's work in the field of kinetography.

Roderyk Lange's task, as revisor, has been to bring the text into line with the many changes that have occurred and are constantly occurring in the interpretation and application of kinetography, while remaining true to the spirit of the original work.

It gives me great pleasure to congratulate Mr. Lange, on behalf of Laban's successors and all enthusiasts of kinetography, upon the high quality of his work. We hope that this book, in its new form, will find the widest possible circulation wherever Laban's kinetography is used.

ROLAND LABAN

Semriach, Austria,
November 1974

CONTENTS

PREFACE TO THE FIRST EDITION

OUR movement and dance notation makes use of the principles on which Beauchamp's and Feuillet's choreography was built up some 300 years ago.*

In a sharp contrast to the fascinating mantic-mystical movement symbolism of thousands of years, Beauchamp and Feuillet created a notation system based on the rational observation of dance movement. The graphic principles which have been kept intact in our notation are the following:

    (*a*) The central line separating movements of the right side of the body from those of the left.

    (*b*) The partitioning of this middle line by bar-strokes indicating a metrical division of time.

    (*c*) The use of directional signs and shape symbols guiding the dancer or moving person in space.

    (*d*) The indication of basic body actions, such as gliding, hitting, etc. by special stress signs.

Feuillet's dances were written along a floor pattern line. We have abandoned this and written the movement sequences along a straight line.

While the old notation was restricted mainly to steps and movements of the legs, we have developed a richer vocabulary which includes the movements of the upper parts of the body and the arms, in accordance with the demands of our contemporary free dance forms and the use of notation in other fields, such as industry. A new analysis of the shapes of the movements which the body follows in space and a special stylisation of the directional signs became necessary.†

In the First Part I have acknowledged the work done by the younger generation of dance notators in the practical development of our dance script after it found its final form.

---

  * Beauchamp's rights as inventor of his dance-notation were recognised by an act of the French parliament in 1666. Feuillet published dances written in this notation around 1700.

  † The essential parts of this analysis and the struggle to establish the new directional signs are described in my book *Choreographie, i.e.* first volume, published by Diederichs, Jena, 1926.

  The final graphic solution was laid down in my book *Schrifttanz* published by Universal Editions, (Vienna 1928).

In this Preface, I wish to acknowledge the great help given to me by pupils and assistants who worked with me at the time of my early experiments, and to other people in various occupations who have taken an interest in my work.

I am thinking especially of the sensitive and inspiring advice received from an excellent dancer, my late friend and colleague, Dussia Bereska. In the earlier part of this century she was the first and only supporter of my work in this field and she predicted the present development and success of notation with acute foresight.

With her fine sense of the flow of movement, Dussia Bereska had a deciding influence on the rhythmical partitioning of Feuillet's metrical bar line intervals. Her suggestion that the symbols might be written in different lengths to indicate the relative duration of each movement was an innovation which is still an outstanding feature of our notation today. I was at that period inclined to condense simultaneous bodily actions around a nucleus having the form of a cross. It is perhaps interesting to mention that this cross sign became later the basic symbol of my effort notation developed for the recording of body actions in industrial operations connected with the notation of psychosomatic states and inner attitudes. I was most encouraged and stimulated by the advice and suggestion of the first script enthusiasts. I will mention here Kurt Jooss, who, after finishing his studies as a pupil of Bereska and myself, surprised us one day with the proposal to duplicate Feuillet's right-left division of the movement sequences. We proceeded then to record the movements of trunk and arms in separate columns instead of inserting them in the upper part of the cross mentioned beforehand. This again has become, with some adaptations, a specific feature of our notation.

How much I am indebted, not so much for technical advice as for the inspiration and insight into choreographic matters given to me by many dancers and dance producers, can be only briefly touched upon here. When I mention a few of these people, it is because I have discussed with them not only the problems of dance script but also of script dance, the interpretation of written dances. Diaghilev and Fokine, and other prominent members of the Russian ballet and other ballet groups, encouraged me in the attempt to create a library of written dances. This is, after all, one of the main uses which the notation has to serve.

I remember also a great number of prominent musicians with whom I had fruitful discussions on this matter. I had the great fortune of having my choreographic creations accompanied by orchestras conducted by Toscanini, Furtwängler, Bruno Walter, Erich Kleiber and other famous musicians, with whom I was able to try out practically the combination of written dance and written music.

My late friend, Siegfried Wagner, the son of Richard Wagner, opened the archives of his father to me, and I discovered to my great surprise the minute care with which this genius composed and notated the movements of all the characters of his casts.

I had the opportunity of reviving his notated movement creations, not only in dance scenes, such as the Tannhäuser Bacchanal, but also in singing parts, for the performances in Bayreuth of several of his music dramas.

When, finally, I express my indebtedness to the scientists, educationists, doctors and industrialists whom I have been able to help with my script in their studies of movement and in its practical application in schools, factories and hospitals, I can do so here in general terms only. My work in all these fields, besides strengthening my conviction of the great practicality and necessity of movement notation, has given me many technical hints which have been incorporated in the final formulation of the script.

Noverre, who in his "ballets d'action" created a free form of stage movement 200 years ago, was an enemy of dance notation because it was mainly used for the description of steps and leg movements. Beauchamp's and Feuillet's initiative has, however, opened much wider horizons than Noverre suspected. We now live to see that the adaptation of dance script to movement in general, as it is attempted in our notation, brings us more friends than enemies.

I am grateful not only to all our friends, but also to our enemies, who have involuntarily helped to overcome the initial weaknesses of the great vision of a literature of movement and dance, with its own language and its own symbolic representation of an important manifestation of the human spirit.

RUDOLF LABAN

Studio Lodge,
Addlestone,
Surrey.
April 1955.

PREFACE TO THE SECOND EDITION

LABAN's initial ideas on a dance script are contained in his book *Choreographie* (Jena, 1926). An already completed outline of his notation system is presented in his publication *Schrifttanz* (Vienna, 1928). This was followed by a span of 28 years of further developments in his kinetography. Over that period Laban's notation system has been applied practically in many fields (education, ergonomic studies, rehabilitation, anthropology, theatre). Yet it was 1956 before Laban decided to publish the outlines of kinetography to document his invention. The result is the present book, which he entitled *Principles of Dance and Movement Notation*.

Of course, the system was constantly developing over the years involving contributions from many people. Textbooks of kinetography written by Laban's followers have appeared: *Labanotation* by Ann Hutchinson, New Directions Books, New York, 1954; *Abriss der Kinetographie Laban* by Albrecht Knust, Das Tanzarchiv, Hamburg, 1956, English translation *ibid* 1958; *Practical Kinetography Laban* by Valerie Preston-Dunlop, Macdonald & Evans Ltd., London 1969 being the main ones. The system has been widened; many analytical problems have been solved following the expansion of kinetography into different specialised areas.

Albrecht Knust has added to the system a big, new chapter on the notation of group movements. His *Encyclopaedia of Kinetography* written mainly in 1946–50 contains a wealth of evidence material (8 volumes, 2400 pages and 20,000 examples) supporting the foundation and rules of kinetography. This work has unfortunately not yet been published.

Shortly before and during World War II some differences arose because of the isolation between the different centres. The unification action carried on after the war by the International Council of Kinetography Laban has now nearly eliminated vital differences existing between the European "Kinetography" and the American "Labanotation." Even if small differences exist between different centres or even individual authors of kinetographic scores, the differing versions can still be read.

What is so remarkable is that the basic principles and the basic signs as invented by Laban have not been changed. They proved to be right and Laban could justifiably state in his book:

"... throughout the whole of this period the fundamental signs that I invented have remained unaltered, which proves that the

underlying principles of the system as first devised by me are sound
and practical " (p. 1)

In publishing this book Laban was first of all concerned with pre-
senting the functional aspect of his notation system. During successive
developments, many new areas and possibilities have been explored but
sometimes one became, possibly, too remote from the intended compact-
ness of the system itself. In this situation, it is surely appropriate that we
should be reminded of the underlying principles of the system. It is this
which makes the book even more relevant today. Developments are
necessary, but they have, of course, to follow consequently and logically
the rules of movement analysis. What is noteworthy is that Laban has
had in mind the general principles underlying any kind of movement
notation (p. 17). He states:

> "Our movement notation is based on the elementary motor
> principles of the human body " (p.11).

Kinetography is a *movement script* which secures the recording of
movement progression. It has to represent the dynamic content inherent
in movement not merely to provide an external picture (p. 4). This
point is actually the asset of Laban's kinetography in comparison with
many of the existing notation systems.

To be able to analyse movement properly one has to think in terms
of movement. Movement is logically structured according to the functions
of the human body in space and time and this has to be understood.
Laban says in conjunction with this:

> "Very often it is not necessary to notate all the effects of movement
> contributing to a final effect " (p. 18).

Many details evolve out of a certain movement context and it is up
to the notator to understand these connections when analysing movement. Therefore kinetography is devised in a way that if one thing is
happening the other is automatically excluded (for example if both legs
are gesturing one cannot put the bodyweight on them. Therefore no
signs will be written in the support columns). This mirrors the functions
of the body in space and time.

Of course, detailed description will be introduced according to the
purpose of the recording. Laban also strongly stresses the necessity of
understanding the signs of the script as having actual counterparts in
real movement possibilities of the human body:

> "The motion characters of the script are compounded according
> to simple orthographical considerations which we have learned to
> appreciate in the long exercise of our experimental notation

activity " (p. 13).

The signs are symbols of a completed logical system and they respond to strict ranges of ideas. Any thoughtless mixing of symbol categories will cause a chain-reaction of inconsistencies. Therefore utmost care should be taken in developing and incorporating new signs:

"A script can become universal only if its basic principles are clearly defined and its essence kept free from contamination " (p. 12).

In preparing the second edition of this book, we have decided to leave Laban's text unchanged, removing or adjusting a few points only which have been outdated or correcting evident mistakes which crept in on a few occasions (*e.g.* "four steps" instead of "five" as indicated by the kinetogram etc.).

The text of the First Part may appear a little old-fashioned and "central European" in style. Also, Laban uses metaphors and anecdotes to colour his discourse (*e.g.* the story of the stars' motion to be notated), but this does not affect the presentation of the principles of his system, which was his concern. For this reason all these digressions have been left as Laban wished them to appear. It gives a personal, and already a period touch to it.

The original text of the whole Second Part has been changed as little as possible. Instead annotations have been provided concurrently with Laban's text. Any differences which have been introduced since Laban's book first appeared have been dealt with. Any of the existing differences between the American (LAB) and European (KIN) schools have been pointed out.

Equipped in this way, the book is more accessible to all practitioners of Laban's system.

RODERYK LANGE

Les Bois,
St. Peter,
Jersey.
November 1974.

First Part

Movement notation and the
fields of its application

MY dance and movement notation has now been before the public since
the 1930s, and I am proud of three facts. The first is that throughout
the whole of this period the fundamental signs that I invented have
remained unaltered, which proves that the underlying principles of the
system as first devised by me are sound and practical. The second is
that quite a large number of people have specialised in the work of
notating dances, exercises and movements of artistic, educational,
industrial and therapeutic nature, and by the practice of this new profession have added a useful store of knowledge and experience to my
first experiments. The third fact, for which I am even more grateful
than I am justly proud, is that I have lived to see several excellent dance
creations of our time preserved for coming generations by being written
down in my notation. In the many fields where this script is used,
improvements have been effected in movement processes and techniques,
together with clarifications of their practical and spiritual content, and
both these desirable improvements have been secured because it has been
possible to study and compare the written scores of recorded movement.

Fully a quarter of a century before the first publication of my system,
I began to experiment with the idea of writing down movements as one
writes words or music. Initially I had nothing more in mind than to
record for my personal use, by a few meaningful scribbles, the steps or
gestures I had invented, mainly for my large orchestral dance compositions.

Later, this embryo notation was made to serve my personal needs on
a much larger scale. Besides scoring numerous opera ballets, my
colleagues and I transcribed into this notation several large communal
dance-plays which were then produced directly from it. In conjunction
with my friend Knust, I wrote the movement score of a festival play for
a thousand performers, and sent the notation to sixty towns from which
the performers at the festival meeting were drawn. As our scores had
been studied by the sixty local groups, the whole thousand people were
able to dance together at the first rehearsal, performing not only the main
motifs, but the whole rather elaborate choreography, lasting two hours,
with very few mistakes or interruptions.

I

A few years later, notations were made of all the job-movements used by the employees of a big estate in their various activities. We surveyed and notated agricultural operations as well as those used in forestry, the mills, and the workshops connected with the estate. The subsequent analysis was used to improve work methods, to train apprentices, and to select operators as well as managers. How is this possible? For the simple reason that movement, when looked at by a trained observer and notator, reveals far more than a purely physical action.

The general public knows next to nothing of the principles of dance notation, or the large-scale applications of this important activity. Except to a few professional practitioners of movement, such as expert dancers, dance teachers, time and motion study engineers, physiotherapists and so on, the idea of a dance notation still appears to the mass of people as strange now as it did to me at the beginning of this century. I feel therefore that I must add an explanatory introduction to this brief exposition of the basic movement notation signs. Let me, then, start from the simplest premises.

Few people, when watching a dancer, will trouble to think much about what is actually happening in their own, or in the dancer's mind. Here, for example, is a child capering about more or less rhythmically, perhaps humming a tune while she does so. One would be inclined, according to temper and circumstances, either to be annoyed at the exhibition or to smile indulgently at the child's antics, and even derive a certain pleasure from them. One might perhaps comment mentally, "How clumsy!" or "How graceful!" A similar reaction might occur if one unexpectedly came upon a crowd of adults amusing themselves by performing their national dances. One might be neither annoyed nor bored, but actually enjoy the sight. Reflecting vaguely on the general mood which the dancers suggest, they might seem to the observer to be gay, or sad, or expressive of more mixed emotions. The dancers might sing while they dance, and it would be understood that they enjoy repeating some simple story of lyrical or dramatic worth. If we are very observant, we go beyond thinking, "How clumsy!" or "How graceful!" and begin to appreciate the appropriateness of the movement invention underlying the idea of the dance. Some performers may indulge in fiercely aggressive steps and body attitudes, while the movements of others may suggest modesty and gentleness. The story may be mimed, but not in a straightforward way as in dumb acting; instead, the moods and events are translated into the language of dance, in which all manner of leaps, twists, turns and other bodily movements occur that no one would use in everyday life.

To observe people dancing for their own enjoyment is a different experience from that derived from attending a ballet executed by professional dancers. First of all, we have paid for our ticket in order to get entertainment, and maybe also some elation, from the show. The spectator of a theatrical dance performance is also more consciously receptive and critical than the casual observer of an impromptu dance. He will still react to clumsiness or grace of movement, and will also appreciate the appropriateness or otherwise of the movement invention to the theme of the dance. But besides this he will expect to be uplifted or enraptured by what he sees. If his desire is not gratified, he leaves the theatre dissatisfied, or at least with the empty feeling of having wasted the evening. Rapture and exultation may of course result from watching amateurs, but not necessarily. The amateurs dance for their own pleasure, and are under no obligation to please anyone but themselves. We see, therefore, that dancing involves invention, execution, and spiritually vitalising effects. Of these three requisites, the first, invention, interests us most at this point. This part of the content of the dance is most subject to human control. Weak and imperfect invention make a good execution, and the resulting exaltation, more difficult for the dancer than does a strong, well-devised composition. The same is true of drama and music. They must be well-invented and clearly composed in order to give the performing artist a suitable basis for his rendering of the work. Up to now dance compositions, unlike poetical and musical compositions, have rarely been written down in an intelligible form. This does not mean that dances have not been well composed. Ballets of extraordinary beauty and vital power have been invented, but, after relatively few performances, have passed into oblivion. When the original inventors and performers had disappeared, the dances could not be reproduced as dramatic and musical works could be from the libretto or the musical score. Put briefly, there is no real literature of dance, although a whole lot of books have been published about dancing in general, and the personalities involved. No faultless descriptions of valuable dances and ballets exist, although the necessity for notated editions of them is obvious to every dancer of distinction.

The several attempts that have been made to write down sequences of steps and gestures in graphical signs have remained relatively unfruitful. Their crudity reminds us of the early stages of script before our present alphabet had been evolved. Rough pictures of objects and hieroglyphs were used to describe the essential events, but to express thought in its subtler nuances requires the phonetic notation of the sounds of speech. We would not know anything about Homer's epics, and other great works of the ancient poets, had they not been written down in phonetic signs; and the same is true of music. Indeed, we do not know anything about the music of the ancients, because no generally acknowledged musical notation of any value existed in antiquity. The invention of the conventional musical signs in which the works of composers have been recorded in the last few centuries, has made it possible for us moderns to perform the works of the great musicians of past ages, which otherwise would long ago have been forgotten. Lacking any system of musical notation, Bach and Beethoven would be no more than silent names to us. Yet nobody knows about the exact movement forms of ballets even of recent origin, though fame proclaims the names of the choreographers, and the appreciation with which their ballets were received in their time.

A new and generally acceptable dance notation comparable with the phonetic alphabet had to be built up. Pictures or diagrams of the external shapes of bodily positions and movements will not serve the ultimate purpose of notating the spiritual content of dances. It is true that one has to show in a notated dance which part of the body has been moved and its position after it has moved. It is also true that the precise time taken for each movement has to be recorded. But all this must be done in such a way that the essential feature of a dance, namely its flow of movement, is described in all its details.

The basic material of dance notation is the motion characters from which it is built up. An example will make clear the dependence of the new dance script on the motion structure. Take the conventional gesture of nodding to express assent; this could be described as "a bending of the head and neck forwards, followed by a relifting of the head into its normal position." One could easily find a graphic sign to depict the external form of this movement, and by adding to it a short or long musical note one could also express the relative speed of the nod. However, in the context of the whole flow of the movement, this nodding might acquire many differing shades of significance. It need not always remain an acquiescent sign of assent. It might express submission, shame, dejection, concentration, misgiving, hostility, and many other feelings. Such significations become clearer if the movements of other parts of the body are marked simultaneously. If, for instance, one or several steps in any direction are indicated at the same time as the nodding, and perhaps other movements as well, such as bending, turning or stretching the arms, hands or trunk, the movement acquires a specific inner significance. When there is a combination of two or more of these movements, the whole chord of several movements will mean something entirely different each time. In most of these cases, the nodding will be divested of its conventional significance, *i.e.* assent, and will become part of a movement expression which cannot be translated immediately into simple words. For the language of movement consists only to a very small extent of conventional signs, replacing, as it were, words and phrases. The main bulk of movement and dance expression consists of motor elements, which can be freely combined to reveal something about the inner state of the moving person. Whether a person uses the language of movement for self-expression, liberation or enjoyment, or for the purpose of communicating with other people, is irrelevant to the present argument.

A generally acknowledged and readable notation of movement, based on the combination of motion characters, is needed today, not only for ballet but for all forms of dancing, and also for dramatic and practical movement studies.

The necessity for an adequate script is more urgent now even than it was because movement study has come to be recognised as a most important feature in industry, education and therapy. In all three fields a rich tradition of movement knowledge is running to waste, since many bodily actions and exercises cannot be preserved. We cannot rely solely on people's memory of movements; nor can the choreographer rely upon his memory, for he might have excellent ideas which he cannot use at the moment, and when the opportunity eventually comes when he can use them, he may find that the ideas have entirely escaped his mind.

Why is it that dancing has not found an adequate and generally accepted form of notation, as have music and poetry? One reason is, doubtless, the lack of a universal movement terminology. Such a terminology, together with a universal notation form, would enable everybody interested in movement to write down, not only occasional ideas for gestures and steps, but also whole ballets. Dance ideas fixed in script could be transmitted to other interested people at any distance in space or time. People in distant countries, as well as future generations, could have the benefit of reading movement ideas and become judges of their artistic or general value. By exchanging movement ideas, tastes and opinions on dance would be clarified, and an apparatus of criticism built up.

The introduction of a dance notation system would mean a revolution in production and performance. Dancers would no longer be restricted to studying and performing their own inventions, or to relying on the imagination of a ballet master who happened to be at hand. Dancers could take their choice from the works of many gifted dance-authors, of whom they had no personal knowledge. Those who invent movement works which they are unable to or do not want to perform themselves could write them down and submit them to the judgment of the entire dancing world.

The two professions, namely the dance-author and the dancer, would probably become separated. It is easy to see that such a separation would provide good solutions to many of the problems of the modern dance stage. The dance public would be much enriched if they were able to see compositions of famous choreographers interpreted by specially talented performers. Anyone who reads press criticisms will agree that any criticism of a theatrical work, no matter whether it is drama, poetry or music, is enormously enhanced in value by consulting the book or score. But the ballet critic is not able to study the composition thoroughly from its score and compare it with the interpretation, at least not yet. He has to concentrate on the performance, and therefore often stresses mere technicalities without appreciating the theme and content of the work. The dance-author, the actual writer of a dance work, would be able to view his work more objectively when it was on paper, and had not as yet been interpreted by an unfortunate dancer who had perhaps spent much hard work staging an invention which might prove unsuitable. A written score would provide greater opportunity for comparing the various parts of a ballet with one another, and for polishing the composition in detail by excising the weaker parts, and by adding necessary variations.

After all, dance as an art cannot be based on spontaneous improvisations only. Movement compositions, as well as poetry and music, have to be carefully constructed and built up according to the general rules of artistic composition. The profound mistake of considering the charming movements of a handsome body as an indication of the artistic value of a dance creation is entirely obsolete today. The development of a movement idea through different logical stages is nowadays the only true criterion of the worth of a dance. Intelligent and tasteful presentation is a factor to be clearly distinguished from creative invention.

A notation based on the combination of motion characters makes it possible to write down all styles of dance, including classical ballet. Ballets of every style use movements built up from the same motor elements. The variety of movement which can be built up from them is almost infinite, and any style with a limited number of variations, whether self-imposed or traditional, must of necessity build its movement forms out of these basic constituents of movement. Just as poetry, in every language, can be written down phonetically, so every stylised movement can be written down "motorically." The motor movement notation is the equivalent of the alphabet. It is, however, only a new principle of notation, not of dance expression or stylisation.

The most widely known product of the art of movement is the ballet. It arose out of the interplay of two distinct desires for showing movement, one leading to dance and the other to mime. Expressed in other words, pure movement as an expression of man's ineffable spirit is here contrasted with movement as a mirror of man's behaviour and actions in life as lived. Movement notation can serve both dance and mime. Historically, dance was probably the first form of movement expression, mime developing later. In rituals and tribal folklore, people tried to realise their higher selves by dramatising what they thought were their chief values and virtues, passing from strength, courage and optimism, to the ideals rooted in enthusiasm, love and sacrifice, and even to religious trance. All the unfathomable impulses and efforts of man became the content of dances. We still see today, in the relics of national dances, the embodiment of tribal ideals, exultation and pride, loveliness, gaiety or langour, cherished differently by each race according to its physical and psychical make-up. Man aspires to be something greater than he is, and knows that he can acquire the greatness that he covets, if only during the imaginative moments when he is lifted above himself in dance. Whether the sincere repetition of such dances produces deeper effects than this, and whether man's spirit is really strengthened by the decision to become his own better self, is an open question. I think we may learn more about this over the years, if we accustom ourselves to notating and pondering the structure of human movements.

At a later stage, dancers tried to represent heroes, gods and kings, and enact the story of their adventures. This enchantment of the personality, as it were by proxy, is without doubt an inner process different from that in pure or personal dancing. When mime became more refined, it dissolved dance movements into conventional gestures, thus disguising man's deeper wish for enhancement. Some two hundred years ago, a revolution against the artificial gesture-language, which had been fostered in the court ballets of the period, led to a fashion for passionate and over-emphatic behaviour on the stage. The names of the great ballet choreographers, Noverre, Vigano, Angolini and others are associated with this revolt. But they could not, or would not, abolish the mime form, and tried to compete with the great tragedy and comedy of the dramatic theatre. Probably plenty of movement still remained in these "ballets d'action," but nothing of it has come down to us because of the lack of an adequate dance notation.

The dance theatre then retired into the sweet coolness of the romantic fairy-tale, in which it still sometimes indulges. Today, there are signs that the struggle for the enhancement of the personality in pure dancing may be revived, but we cannot follow up the actual history of dance styles and dance contents, because we have inherited no real "motor picture" of them. The inaccessible and valuable content of movement and dance, which cannot be explained in words, needs some form of description, and this can only be based on the motor facts of bodily action.

The dancer who wishes to express an inner state of mind or mood has to use the motor elements in definite order. Dance, like music, has its harmony, which does not consist only of soft, sweet expressions, but embraces all motor elements, including dissonant elements. It is a matter of personal taste whether a modern dance author breaks down sweetness into discord, or liberates grotesqueness by leading it into well-shaped harmony. Most modern choreographers use every facet of human experience, with the obvious intention of awakening in the spectator a heightened sense of the tension in life. This enlivening of the spectator by the free use of the innumerable shades and variations of life tension is perhaps the most valuable aspect of pure dancing on the stage at the present day. Yet whatever content of dance the composer may choose, and whatever style of presentation he may favour, he cannot really succeed in transmitting it to future generations if he does not build it with the bricks of the elementary motor faculties of the human body which remain unchanged throughout all ages. The procedure of the dance composer must be similar to that of the poet, who, no matter what his native tongue or subject of discourse may be, must build his words on the simplest phonetic faculties of the human voice. Although it is obvious that the words and phrases of the language of movement (for so the shapes and rhythms of dance may be called) have no determinable verbal meaning, they are nevertheless subject to an ordered principle, namely the balanced flow and harmony of movement. The structure and function of the body limits the number of movements which the human being can perform. We are not able to fly like birds, nor do we normally jump about on our heads as some clowns may do in the circus, and we suffer many other limitations because of the structure and function of our bodies and minds; but we have the instinct of self-preservation, and therefore prefer movements which are conducive to physical and mental safety rather than those which would endanger body and soul. We are proud of our erect carriage, which both symbolises and guarantees our supremacy over the beasts; we like to keep a balance, and to use our "tentacles," the arms and hands, to satisfy our needs and desires. We attract, and are attracted by, that which we love, and repulse, and are repulsed by, anything hostile. In sleep, we close our eyes and relax our muscles, while we are full of interest and activity when awake. Our facial expression and bodily carriage can indicate morosity or cheerfulness according to our inner mood, but we can also feign moods, and hide our thoughts behind our movements, just as we can feign the loss of our normal balance in miming a drunkard's gait. We can be sincere or false in movement, and, curiously enough, it is by our movements that people are often made aware of our insincerity.

All this a good observer is able to write down in motor symbols. Movement events in our inner and outer life have a spiritual significance, and can be rendered in movement notation with more exactitude than when they are described in words. A skilled reader of movement notation can not only understand what the body of the dancer does, but he can shudder or smile on deciphering the mental and emotional contents of the symbols. Just as a skilled musician is able to hear with the inner ear the melody as he scans it in a musical score, so a skilled dancer can see with his inner eye the movements of the human body while reading the dance notation.

The striking thing is that the notation consists solely of a few signs, representing the elementary motor faculties of man, combined in various ways. The two score letters of the alphabet, with punctuation marks, are sufficient in most languages to write down all our thoughts. Barely two score signs are needed to depict all our movements, and to create permanent records of the whole content of ballets and dances. It must be stressed that we see not signs of shapes only, but also signs of rhythms. The latter are often considered solely as audible phenomena, an assumption which is certainly not true in dancing. By looking at any poetry of movement other than European ballet, the folk-lore of remote races, for example, one becomes intensely aware of the importance of rhythm in dance expression. It is true that this rhythm is usually made audible by the accompanying drumming or music, or, rather, that audible and visible rhythms become a unity in dance. The legend that the Indian___

God Shiva danced the "Tandava" (Dance of Creation) to the rhythm of "The Sacred Drum" clearly reveals the part which rhythm plays in the movement content. The sacred drum is the symbol of that eternal vibration which has been thought to be the creative power ruling the world. The shapes of dance movements are visual patterns, which have in their flux and flow a visible rhythm. The spectator recognises the counterplay of definite mental states of balance and harmony as he watches the external shapes and rhythms of the dancer's body.

Javanese dancing originated from the shadow-plays, in which the contours of mobile marionettes are projected on a screen. In the drama, the puppets do not represent people but are symbols of human qualities and moral capacities. It is perhaps of interest to remark that dance and drama performed by living beings was introduced in Java as a spectacle as recently as two hundred years ago. It was a long time before the Javanese acquired a taste for watching living performances, and many of them still prefer the shadow-plays of their puppets. Is it because these shadows show purer movement than the living performer? The Javanese did, however, dance by themselves before they became reconciled to dance as a spectacle. If one dances alone one cannot see one's own movements, but one feels the motor action stimulating rhythmic vibration, and, added to it, the sense of the shape and pattern which the body draws in the air.

The sense of activity which one gets from dancing by oneself is essentially different from the relatively passive receptivity of the spectator of dancing. This explains why dance was for a long time in human history— or rather in human pre-history—a paramount means of education and therapy. In order to take advantage of the beneficial vibrations experienced in the shapes and rhythms of dance, the dance teacher or practitioner has to know more about the vibrations of movements and the basic motor rules which they obey.

Knowledge of this kind is in my opinion the best introduction to creating and understanding movement notation. As a basic motor script, move-ment notation can have various purposes. Some time ago, time and motion study used in industry to regulate working movement had to be amended as a result of investigations then being made into human effort. For this purpose dance notation proved to be a most appropriate aid. In assessing the physical and mental capacities of a person for a specific task, his habitual movement forms can give clear indications of his ability or otherwise to perform it, and, with other tests, build up a complete picture of his personality; and from the analysis of the movement notation he can easily be placed into a suitable job.

Our movement notation is based on the elementary motor principles of the human body, and can be applied to a larger range of activities, which in turn has assisted its rapid dissemination. I have in justice to speak of *our* notation, for though I discovered the principles and invented the basic symbols, I could never have established it unaided, and successfully developed the final version. The struggle for the recognition of the pressing necessity for a basic dance notation serving all movement purposes is centred round a few people who are best called movement notators. The present notation form has been built up and tried out mainly in Europe and America. There are professional notators and interested persons all over the world, but they are all working in connection with one of three main groups.

The senior notator is Albrecht Knust, who has recorded the results of his extensive investigations into the motor rules of human body functions in a standard work of eight volumes, which still awaits publication. I have to acknowledge here Knust's generosity in allowing me to use his rich collection of basic notation examples in preparing this book. Knust has transcribed in our notation a number of ballets and many choral dance works besides a host of folk dances, some of them of exotic origin, from many countries.

Ann Hutchinson, and her staff of the Dance Notation Bureau in New York, have the great advantage of witnessing in that cauldron of all races a large number of dances in every style. The most active American stage dancers have taken up our notation as an instrument urgently needed in the profession, and this is largely due to the work of Ann Hutchinson. It may be mentioned here that the American group calls our system "Labanotation."

In England, Lisa Ullmann, and Sigurd Leeder in Switzerland, together with an appreciable circle of fellow movement notators, are spreading the use of the script in general and theatrical education. They emphasise the value of notating movement exercises and educational dance studies. All active notators are used to stressing the importance of notation as a means of keeping choreographic invention free from distortion by busy imitators. Besides the practical issues connected with the copyright of dance works, the use of notation has the effect of preserving the integrity of original works.

It is in this sphere of aesthetic property rights that the notators' fight has been fiercest, with the result that today our notation is officially recognised as a means of obtaining copyright for works on the art of movement.

A script can become universal only if its basic principles are clearly defined and its essence kept free from contamination. It is inevitable that some small differences should have appeared in the way of writing. The two main centres, the Dance Notation Bureau in New York and the Kinetographisches Institut in Essen, have developed the notation according to their particular needs, and since means of communication were lacking during the war years, it is only comparatively recently that the opportunity has arisen to discuss these divergencies and to try to resolve them. This process of integration is now well under way, but the student should be aware of the slight variations so that he experiences no difficulty when reading a script whatever its source.

There are one or two minor variations which occur only when the movement is very stylised, or when it is necessary to write in minute detail. One is worth mentioning by way of example: the sign descriptive of a very light movement. All the variations are still based fundamentally on the original sign which I proposed twenty-five years ago, namely a comma, but in Europe it has been developed into an angular comma, while in America it has been rounded. Such small differences exist even in the ordinary spelling of words in the two continents. However, everybody is still able to read both versions.

One of the second generation of movement notators, Valerie Preston-Dunlop, to whom I am indebted for her help in arranging the examples in this book, has undertaken the meritorious task of acting as a communication officer between the various Notation Centres.

The special application which movement notation has found in industry has developed from the fact that dancers frequently handle objects and tools, *i.e.* stage properties, when on the stage. The close connection between the movements made when handling stage properties and those used in industrial operations is obvious. It was therefore not difficult to describe the workmen's task-movements in our notation, notwithstanding the differences between the stage and the industrial scripts. An essential point here is that the rhythmic-dynamic signs of my script had to be dovetailed into a more elaborate form for the special industrial purpose, where scientific analysis of the movement is the first and last consideration. The rhythmic-dynamic signs in stage script, whose aim is to describe rather than to investigate, could be kept more simple than the same sort of signs in industry, where they are used for analysing and notating the efforts of workers performing specific tasks, or undergoing movement tests, the tests being made to determine the competence of the worker to perform a specific job.

Since the late 1940s, Frederic Charles Lawrence, the eminent business consultant, co-author with myself of the book *Effort* (MacDonald & Evans Ltd., London, 1947, 2nd ed. 1974), has introduced our specialist notation form into industry as a tool of the effort-assessor.

The psychological factors involved in movement notation, whether dealing with artistic work on the stage or with training in trade schools, technical institutes and factories, have made it possible to extend the use of the script to psycho-therapeutic investigation.

These fascinating sidelines branching off from dance notation have to be mentioned here in order to assign all the various applications to their right places. A person once asked me whether my notation might soon not be used for recording the movements of the stars in the sky. I was glad to assure him that no such invasion into the astronomer's domain was contemplated, for the simple reason that our movement notation could be used only to describe and analyse human movement. Still, the continuous emergence of brilliant new stage stars might for all I know offer the movement notator of the future a welcome subject for a fascinating whole-time study.

The motion characters of the script are compounded according to simple orthographical considerations which we have learned to appreciate in the long exercise of our experimental notation activity. Knust has collected in his great standard work some 20,000 basic movement graphs. This should not frighten anyone, for a modern dictionary contains some 40,000 to 50,000 words with explanations.

Such graphs represent something like the sound combinations of language which constitute words. In the examples given in this book I can give less than a hundredth part of Knust's collection, but I hope that despite its fragmentariness it will provide an introductory vocabulary of use to the ever-increasing number of friends of our notation, both those who are professionally connected with the art of the dance and also the ever-growing number of dance lovers and those interested in this new field of aesthetics and harmony.

Second Part

*Introducing the necessity for thinking in terms of movement and
the explanations of the graphs*

MOVEMENT notation is a guide to the performance of definite movements
depicted in a series of graphic symbols. The writing and reading of
notation necessitates an exact knowledge of the signs by which the details
of the flow of movement in the body are indicated.

Movement notation gives therefore more than a description in words
could offer. Verbal explanation is bound to be much too long-winded
for the stimulation of immediate performance. The reading of the notation
graphs involves a certain amount of spelling of the successive details,
but this spelling has to become fairly automatic, so that the whole
complex of a motif is almost instantaneously absorbed and translated
into action. The feel of movement preceding the performance is a mental
act.

It is perhaps useful to stress the complexity of trying to explain a movement in words. Even with very simple motions, and even if they are
described in a kind of telegram-style, it is very difficult to express the
essentials of a movement precisely. Take, for instance, a "step." We have
to ask immediately which leg is stepping, and arrive perhaps at the
statement that it is a "right step." Considering next the direction of
space into which the step is done, we might expand this to a "right step
forward." We have to state now whether it is a large or a small step,
and decide finally that it is a "right step forward of normal size"—which
means that it is neither excessively long nor particularly short. Now
comes the duration of the step. It is possible to perambulate in a slow
dignified manner or to hurry hastily along, almost running. But this is
not all; time-durations are relative to one another, and we have to know
whether the step in question is quicker or slower than the other steps
preceding or following it. If we know that it is quicker, we also want to
know how much quicker it is. Our verbal description will then have to
be expanded in the following way: "right step forward of normal size,
twice as quick (or slow) as the preceding (or following) steps." We are not
yet at the end of our enquiry, because it has still to be said whether the
step ends in a standing position on a bent or a normally stretched leg, or
whether the leg is elevated on the ball of the foot or on the toe. When
this information is added to our description, it will in the chosen case run

as follows: "Right step forward of normal size and half the duration of the previous one, landing on the ball of the foot with stretched knee."

When we consider that all this can be expressed in a notation graph by *one single sign* or motion character, we will understand that the eye and the mind can absorb this picture not only much more quickly, but also as a single incentive to perform the movement without that mental reflection which is detrimental to spontaneous action.

One step is, of course, only a tiny part of a movement motif, in which several steps of different character might occur, accompanied perhaps by simultaneous arm gestures and expressive positions of the head and the hands. It is quite impossible to express in words the subtle co-ordination and relationships of several movements otherwise than in a very long-winded sentence. Nobody would be able to condense what he has read into a sudden and clear perception of the movement, inaugurating its immediate performance.

A motif, that is, a sequence of motions, is depicted in notation on a graph, condensed on the paper into a relatively small space which can be seen in one glimpse; and after a short training of the eye, such a graph can be simultaneously absorbed and interpreted.

The essential requirement for this is to learn to think in terms of movement. If it is desired to give a short survey of the principles of dance and movement notation, it is necessary to awaken this sort of thinking in the reader's mind. In my experience, the simple tabulation of the symbols, that is, the mere presentation of an alphabet of the letters of the language of movement, cannot serve this purpose adequately.

The presentation of the principal symbols of notation attempted in the following sections of this booklet might make uninspiring reading as far as the text is concerned. It is impossible to give such an explanation any literary charm. The strange world of the logic of movement has to be elucidated in its own terms and without even using the professional jargon of the dancer or the industrialist.

The essential text of the second part of this book consists, therefore, of the graphs of movements and motifs, while the verbal description of a few fundamental movement ideas and their symbols has to remain rather accidental.

There exist detailed orthographic conventions of writing used in the theatre, the factory, the school and in remedial work. Different movement motifs stand in the foreground of interest in each one of these professional applications of the script. It is true that aesthetic harmony, economy of effort or psychological significance can be found in any application of the notation to a special purpose, but the stress on one or another of the characteristics of movement will change with the different final aims of the various occupations for which the recording is used.

We do not deal here with these specialised orthographies, but with the general principles underlying any kind of movement notation.

Before turning to the explanations of the movement graphs, some of these general principles will be briefly mentioned.

The flow of movement is felt in the body as a minor or major motion of the muscles of one or several parts of the body, and sometimes of the whole body.

This flow is seen by an observer in its result or effect as a slight or large displacement in space of one or several parts of the body, and sometimes of the whole body. What is first noticed by the observer and felt by the moving person is the slight movement in the spine, the legs and the arms. It is not at once realised where to or in what direction the movement leads. We are soon interested in the *duration* of the movement, which is represented in notation by a duration line. Duration lines of equal length signify an equal time duration.

Time units can be marked on a central staff line, and in reading the notation, it can be estimated how each movement of a part of the body lasts one or several time units. When the duration line ends the movement finishes also. It may re-start at a later moment.

Sometimes the movements of several parts of the body overlap, and several movements then have certain time units or counts in common.

In notation we have also to consider the effects of an initial impulse, which will be briefly characterised here.

We can discern:

The *fundamental movement* of a definite part or parts of the body.

The *tactile effect*, if the end of a moving part touches an object, *e.g.* if the foot (end-articulation of the leg) touches the ground, or if the hand (end-articulation of the arm) touches an object or person.

The *support effect*, when a foot, hand or any other part or parts of the body carries the weight.

The *prehensile effect* or grasp, *e.g.* when the hand grips an object. The prehensile effect can be combined with the support effect, *e.g.* in grasping the branch of a tree or a rung of a ladder and hanging on to it by the hands and arms.

Several subsequent support effects of any kind combine into the *ambulatory effect*, *e.g.* when two or more steps are taken, or several ladder rungs are hung on to, one after another. In any ambulatory effect each progress from one support to the next has its own tactile or prehensile sub-section.

The *saltatory effect* arises from the flinging of the body from one place to the other, whereby the body is thrown into the air and remains for a short time without support, *e.g.* in a leap or jump or in acrobatic turns in the air. Every saltatory effect ends in a landing, *i.e.* in the regaining of a support. Producing the saltatory effect or fling involves an elastic rebounce.

The *rebounce effect* is also noticeable, in contrast to the touch (tactile effect), as a thrusting or pushing away of an object or a person.

The *swinging or pendulum effect* arises from the passive hanging down of one or several limbs, or of the whole body hanging on hands or feet, etc. In this case a wave of movements above the passively hanging part sets the latter into a swinging motion.

Very often it is not necessary to notate all the effects of movements contributing to a final effect.

This is, for instance, the case in ordinary stepping and walking, where the preparatory lifting and shifting of the stepping leg is omitted and only the final effect of the transference of the weight support is recorded.

In the more elaborate steps of dancing, which gain their expressive quality from the varying combination of various preparatory and intermediate effects, all these details must of course be notated.

There is here an important difference between movement notation and dance notation. This applies also, of course, to the detailed notation of the various movement effects in arm gestures, which are quite different in working actions and in dance movements.

SECTION A

The notation of the flow* of movement in the body and the duration of movement

1. THE symbols of movement notation are inscribed in a system of three parallel lines, the staves. It is useful to position the staves vertically in writing the script, because an essential feature of the script thus remains constantly before the eye. This feature is that the central staff line divides the writing space into two halves; in the left half are notated the movements of the left side of the body, while the right half is reserved for movements of the right side of the body†.

Exceptions to this are the movements of the trunk and its main carrier the spine, which are written on both sides, immediately adjacent to and outside the two outer staff lines‡.

Movement impulses for the lower and upper extremities issue from the spine. Nerve tracks issuing from the left side of the spine convey the movement impulses to the left side extremities, and likewise where the right leg and arm are concerned.

2. Spine and trunk movements often precede leg and arm movements. In graph 2 a spine and trunk movement initiates a simultaneous movement of both arms. Leg movements (*see* graphs 3, 4, 5) are inserted within the staves, while arm movements are written outside the staves (*see* graph 4), farther away from them than the spine-trunk movements.

3. A spine-trunk movement (written on both sides of the staves) precedes a right leg movement. The left leg, supporting the weight of the body, is immobile. A nought is inserted adjacent to the central staff line to signalise a pausing of the flow of movement in the left leg§.

---

*Flow meaning the general flux of movement, progression, continuity.

†General note. Now a double bar line is always needed to indicate the start of action. (KIN at the beginning of each column) ⫼

‡The two columns immediately to the right and left of the stave are now reserved for the movements of the *upper part of the body*. This technical term includes movements around and/or in the spine involving the shoulder girdle, or part of it, but excluding the hip joints. They are written with direction signs on both sides of the stave. Movements involving the whole trunk include the hip joint and are written with ▯ on one side of the stave only. This applies also to parts of the trunk.

§The nought indicating the pausing is called a *pause* or *retention sign*.

4. This graph shows a movement of the spine followed by simultaneous right leg and arm movements, which are again each of a duration of two time units. The movements of the trunk and the extremities overlap in time and move together for one time unit. The body weight is carried by the immobile left leg.

5. Shows the same movement as in (4), but a left leg movement follows the spine movement. The body weight is carried by the immobile right leg.

6. No spine movement precedes the independent right step, *i.e.* a taking over of the weight of the body from the left leg, which has initially carried the body weight after a transitory right leg gesture. In this graph the transference of the weight from the left to the right leg has the same duration of one time unit as the succeeding left step, and so on.

The stepping movement is written in the support column adjacent to the central staff line.

7. Gaps between steps—here of one time unit—signify a jump or leap. This becomes still more obvious if simultaneous right and left leg gestures are written in this gap, so that the body is evidently without support during this time unit.

8. Here are shown the same gaps between subsequent supports as in the previous graph 7. The pause in the movement of the stepping leg is indicated by a nought or zero after the step. It prolongs the support of the body weight by the stepping leg in immobility until the other leg takes the weight over. No jump, of course, is made.

9. At the end of the two independent movements of the arms a sign for a prehensile or grasping movement of the hands (x) is added. Movements of the hand are notated a further small distance away from the staves, and have their own duration line, which is in the present example much shorter than the main arm movement. No touch of an object is indicated, so that the contraction of the hand and fingers is an expressive movement and not connected with an objective action.

10. By the same contraction sign, bendings or contractions of the spine, of the legs or the arms can also be indicated.

11. The stretching or widening of a movement is indicated by an N-like sign. This sign is also used when the fingers of the hand are widely spread. See the last spreading movement of the left hand.

The sign is now written
Ⱶ

12. Three steps of normal size are followed by three short steps and then by three long steps.

13. A horizontal bow connecting two parts of the body indicates touch. Here the hands touch one another, both in active movement.

14. The right hand moves actively to touch the left hand, which remains passively immobile wherever it is actually positioned. This passivity is indicated by a dotted duration line in the left-hand column in this graph.

15. Both hands grip one another, both with active movement. The grip or grasp sign is the narrow sign (x) within the bow of touch.

16. The right hand touches and grips the left hand in active movement. The left hand remains passive, immobile.

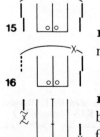

17. Rebouncing movements of the arms. The right bounces from narrow to wide and back to narrow, the left from wide to narrow and back to wide. Both movements are very quick.

18. With an active movement of the spine both arms swing out passively. In the second half the passive right leg is set swinging by a trunk impulse.

19. The parts of the arm move successively:—

> 1st articulation of arm: shoulder—sign: 1 short inclined stroke
>
> 2nd articulation of arm: elbow—sign: 2 short inclined strokes
>
> 3rd articulation of arm: wrist—sign: 3 short inclined strokes
>
> 4th articulation of arm: hand—sign: 4 short inclined strokes

All affixed to short duration lines.

When the parts of the arm move in this order an arm gesture acquires a fluent expression.

19a. The succession of the movements of the parts of the arm in the above order can be expressed in notation by a V-like *succession sign* inserted before the arm-gesture duration strokes.

20. The parts of the leg move successively:

> 1st articulation of the leg: hip—sign: 1 short horizontal stroke
>
> 2nd articulation of the leg: knee—sign: 2 short horizontal strokes
>
> 3rd articulation of the leg: ankle—sign: 3 short horizontal strokes

4th articulation of the leg: foot—sign: 4 short horizontal strokes

All crossing short duration lines.

When the parts of the leg are moved in this order, the leg gesture acquires a fluent expression.

20a. The succession of the movements of the parts of the leg in the above order can be expressed in notation by a V-like *succession sign* inserted before the leg-gesture duration stroke.

Note that the signs for the sub-sections of the legs are the same for the right and left sides. For the arms, they are different for the right and left sides.

now used by LAB only, the KIN symbol is V)
See also Nos. 19a *and* 24.

21. The parts of the spine move successively.

Order: Movement of the lower part of the spine (pelvis area), indicated by the centre of weight or gravity sign, a bow or square with a black disc in it; followed by movement of the upper part of the spine (chest area), indicated by a bow or square with a white disc in it.

The new centre of gravity sign is ●

● pelvis sign
◉ chest sign

both symbols are written in the first column outside the stave (on one side only).

21a. The above order in the succession of the movements of the parts of the spine can be expressed in notation by the V-like succession sign.

22. The sub-sections of the spine—and with them the parts of the trunk—can move separately. Here the lower (pelvis) area moves alone.

22a. The chest area of the spine and tunk moves alone.

23. The whole torso moves as a whole without articulation, followed by an independent head movement. Sign for the head, a capital "C" (from *Caput* = "head" in Latin).

Note: To graphs 21 and 23 alternative signs used in dance notation for pelvis, chest and torso are added.

only now used.

24. The parts of the arms and legs move less frequently in the reversed order of succession, which is then notated by an inverted succession sign (∧).

The vertical bow joining the articulation of successively performed body movements indicates smooth transitions (*see* graphs 19, 24, 25).

25. Any other order of independently moving parts of arms and legs is of course possible. For example, in graph 25, the order of the motions in the parts of the arms is wrist, shoulder, elbow, while the order of the motions of the parts of the left leg is ankle, hip, knee.

Note: No succession sign can be written for irregular movement sequences of parts of the extremities.

26. Shows the notation of fingers by dots inserted into the sign of the 4th arm articulation, the hand.

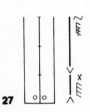

(*a*) = thumb.
(*b*) = index finger.
(*c*) = middle finger.
(*d*) = ring finger.
(*e*) = little finger.

This order results from Laban's dance style in the period when the rudiments of the script were being established. Now the accepted order is:
(*a*) little finger
(*b*) ring finger
(*c*) middle finger
(*d*) index finger
(*e*) thumb

LAB way of writing is

thumb

little finger, etc.

27. This graph shows, in the first motion, a shorter arm gesture with inverted succession of parts, in which the hand is narrowed in a grip-like fashion (all fingers bent); in the second motion, a longer arm gesture with everted succession of parts, in which three fingers of the hand, *i.e.* thumb, index finger and middle finger are widened (stretched).

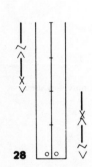

28. In the first motion everted succession of arm articulations is combined with a stretching or widening of the right arm.

In the second motion inverted succession of arm articulations is combined with bending or narrowing of the right arm.

In the third motion everted arm articulation is combined with bending or narrowing of the left arm.

In the fourth motion inverted arm articulation is combined with stretching or widening of the left arm.

Note: The same combination of everted and inverted articulation successions with either narrowing or widening is also possible for the legs.

The fundamental bodily actions of scooping, gathering (in contrast to strewing), and scattering (or pushing away) are based on such combinations of narrow and wide extensions of the limbs with definite orders of succession of the articulations.

29. The graph shows both hands making a fist in the first motion, and spreading hands and fingers very wide in the second motion.

Note: This strong concentration and extension is indicated by a double narrow sign and a double wide sign.

The double wide sign now used is

30. The head can also be held either very low (narrowly) by bending and pressing the chin to the chest or very high (widely), as in the colloquial expression "with the nose in the air."

Following the consideration that the head cannot really become *narrower* or *wider* as a body part, a new way of writing has been established for these movements:

Duration strokes can be added if these actions, written in 29 and 30, are performed very slowly.

The double narrow and double wide signs are also used as prefixes to any kind of movement, as for instance for the indication of very short or very long steps.

31. The touch sign—a horizontal bow—is also used to indicate the touching of the ground. In graph 31 an arm gesture is seen, in which the hand touches the ground; this is shown by the touching bow leading from the hand to the support column. No weight is transferred to the hand or arm in this case, nor in the following graph 32.

32. The left knee touches the ground, but without really kneeling on it.

33. Here the weight of the body is transferred to both hands and the head.

This is now written as

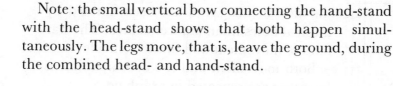

Note: the small vertical bow connecting the hand-stand with the head-stand shows that both happen simultaneously. The legs move, that is, leave the ground, during the combined head- and hand-stand.

34. The weight reposes on both feet, while the arms perform gestures consisting of an everted succession of their articulations.

35. Kneeling on the right knee, while the fingers of both hands touch the ground, without, however, carrying weight. The left leg moves away in a wide movement.

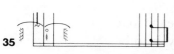

36. Hand-stand on both hands. A right-leg gesture connected with a contraction of the trunk leads to a standing on the right foot and then on both feet. While the feet take over the weight, the trunk and both arms stretch widely.

37. The body lies on the right shoulder and hip, *i.e.* on the right side. Note the connecting bow as a sign of simultaneity. The left hand touches the left knee.

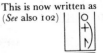

This is now written as
(*See* also 102)

37

38. Standing on both feet, followed by sitting, and then by lying down on the whole torso (hip-shoulders, *see* graph 23); in the lying position both legs are stretched far out.

38

39. Note the repetition sign for the movement sequence, which consists of two equal (=) signs, one on the left at the bottom and the other on the right at the top of the movement notation.

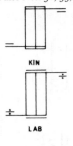

The new repeat signs are
(*See* also Nos. 98, 99, 100)

KIN

LAB

Motif 39 forms a sequence of arm gestures, steps and a jump (both legs gesturing away from the ground) and a few further steps with trunk and arm motions; the rhythm of the movements 34–39 has been notated by musical notes in an adjacent stave. The bar lines of movement and music coincide.

Both movement and the accompaniment by music are repeated in graph 39.

It is possible to write dances parallel to the accompanying music, or to accompany notated movement by a drum or some other percussion instrument while reading the rhythm from the movement score.

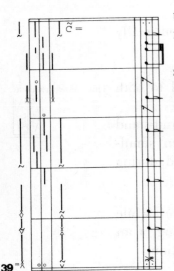

39

Within the body movement several rhythms can appear, each one followed by different parts of the body. In this sense the body is to be considered as a kind of orchestra, in which arms, legs, trunk, head, hands, shoulders and all the other articulations play their parts.

In Section A we have dealt with "narrow" and "wide" movements without taking into consideration the many possible turnings and revolutions of the limbs or of the whole body towards the various regions of space.

Downwards, towards the ground, and upwards in the air are two of the regions of space that must be considered, but there are many more; in movement the most obvious ones are the sideways direction (opening-closing) and the forwards and backwards directions (advancing-retiring).

Changes of front, as in turning to the right or to the left until one faces in a new direction, necessitate the indication of such movements with special signs.

From the weight-level and directional viewpoint, all movements can be understood as a series of definite positions in space. This applies not only when a simple turning towards a new direction is involved, but also when, in a series of movements, the limbs or the whole body are turned into many of the different possible directions during the motif. This will be best understood by comparing the possible body positions in space with those of statues, which may be standing; kneeling, sitting, lying or even, in jumping, flying through the air; in doing so they, with their limbs, may point to any of the regions of space surrounding them.

This comparison with statues in their various positions is applicable mainly to the art of dancing. The everyday activities of contemporary man are in general much less "plastic." But in sports, games, hunting climbing and sailing and also in certain working activities a great amount of movement plasticity can still be observed.

In dancing, as well as in everyday gait, in work and in the manner of carrying the body, a great variety of movement levels is noticeable; some people bend their back and knees habitually, while others walk and move in an erect fashion, as if stretching upwards.

These differences between the habitual weight-levels of the body are of interest to the movement notator.

The direction into which every single movement leads can be compared to the "pitch" of a melody. The detailed prescription of these directions will be discussed in the next Section.

SECTION B

The notation of weight-level and the directions of movement

DURATION strokes broadened into blocks of three different shades indicate three levels of height towards which a movement can be orientated.

40 (*a*). This shading of the block-sign by strokes means a *high* level. The example shows: Standing elevated on the balls of the feet, with straight knees. Both arms are raised high.

(*b*) Shading by blackening the whole block means *deep* level. The example shows: Standing on the whole feet with lowered (bent) knees. Both arms are directed downwards by the sides of the body.

(*c*) Shading with a dot in the centre of the block means *medium* level. The example shows: Standing on the whole feet with straight knees.

41. In graph 41, two sets of directional signs are shown.

The larger shaded blocks, of different shapes, can be drawn longer or shorter according to the varying durations of the movements represented by them.

The smaller, pin-shaped signs point to definite directions, but have no time value and remain, therefore, always of the same size.

The block-signs, which have been developed from broadened duration strokes, are compound signs containing combined indications of the level, the direction and the duration of a movement. They are called motion characters (the letters of the lan-

"Motion characters" are now named "direction signs."

guage of movement). Written into the various columns of the staves, they indicate complex movement actions for each part of the body.

The blocks are of four different shapes:

The rectangular shape (*see* graphs 40*a*, *b*, *c*) indicates the vertical direction which is called "place." This can be low, medium or high.

The pointer shape, almost like an index finger, indicates forward movements when pointing to the top of the vertically arranged staves, and backward movements when pointing to the bottom of the staves.

The arrowhead shape (truncated triangle), pointing to the left or to the right of the writing space, indicates movements to the left or right in a sideways direction.

The diagonal corner shape indicates movements in intermediate directions: forwards-right, backwards-right, backwards-left and forwards-left.

In the centre of graph 41 are written the rectangular signs indicating the three levels, high, low, and middle or medium (*see* graph 40). The spot on the floor under the centre of gravity of the body is called "place."

Theoretically any one of the duration strokes in Section A could be replaced by one or several of the motion characters of graph 41; in this way an indication of the direction and level of the movement would be given. However, the exact control of the space element allows the definition of certain significant patterns of movement which have to be discussed.

Such patterns are:

Floor patterns, built up from *steps* of definite directions.

Air patterns, designed by arm gestures into definite regions of space.

Changes of front, facing towards varying space directions, as a result of turns, or runs along circular or curved pathways.

Variations of motifs based on significant changes of bodily positions in space. The positions of the articulations of the spine and extremities and of their turnings towards definite regions of space are expressed by motion characters and pin-signs.

An important conception of the space orientation of extremities is the hub or centre of direction. An arm movement forward will lead shoulder high (the natural level of the hub), in front of the shoulder, while a leg movement forward will lead at hip height in front of the hip. In this way many forward directions exist, each one "in front" of the joint which is the hub of the directional movement. The shoulder is the hub of the arm, the elbow is the hub of the forearm, the wrist is the hub of the hand; and similarly the hip is the hub of the leg, the knee of the lower part of the leg, and the ankle of the foot.

As will be shown, the exact indication of movement directions offers the possibility of recording a rich variety of movement patterns.

Each example shown in Section B allows almost unlimited variations, which can only be briefly indicated in this short survey of the principles of dance and movement notation.

A very large number of possible combinations of linear and plastic patterns can be built up from directional indications. Floor patterns of steps can be combined with air patterns. Both floor patterns and air patterns can contain twists and turns, or be performed in straight directions. Combined linear patterns can become plastic, if the simultaneous movements follow different directions. The pattern of movement can be interrupted at any place by pauses in definite positions. Such positions, in which the movement stops, can be assumed by the whole body or by any single part of it. Variations in the length of the directional signs allow any part of a pattern to be speeded up or slowed down, so that the pattern can be performed with any imaginable rhythm. Indications of deviated or diverted direction can give the pattern a great range of sizes and variations in shape. Manifold possibilities exist of touching, gripping, or carrying objects or a person, either while stationary or while moving along a floor-pattern path; these actions can be combined with suitable air patterns.

These various combinations of movement have their own logic; the possible variations are restricted in several ways. The human body can hover in the air only for a very short moment, during a jump. The body or its limbs frequently form a kind of obstacle on a directional path, and this obstacle has to be circumvented. The smaller articulations of the body, as, for instance, the fingers, have their own restricted orbit of movement. These logical considerations of what is possible or impossible for a normally functioning body are reflected in certain rules of the graphical representation of movement.

The graphs of Section B show some typical combinations of directional indications.

42

42. Steps in different directions create *floor patterns*. The front of the body remains facing the same direction. The steps are all at a medium weight-level.

With each step a new *stance* is reached from which, as a *centre*, the direction of the next step is reckoned.

In the first right step, the weight will be transferred to the right foot; a left step then crosses from this new stance-centre diagonally right and forwards. Again a new stance is reached, from which the next step forward is made with the right foot, and so on, until the last left step returns near to the starting place. If the steps become increasingly shorter, say: 1st step very long (double length), 2nd step long, 3rd step normal extension, 4th step short, 5th step very short (half the 4th), and 6th, 7th and 8th steps extremely short, a successively narrowing pathway would be formed.

A successively widening pathway would be formed through increasingly lengthening steps (starting with very short ones). A great number of variations of floor patterns can be described through the combinations of steps of different directions and extensions.

Now the starting position is always enclosed in the stave as follows

Note: In this sequence of steps the changing of the direction of the fourth step (from right diagonal forwards to left diagonal forwards) would alter the floor pattern into a circular path. The method of describing the following of a circular path with a continuous change of front is shown in graph 55.

43. Arm or leg gestures made in different directions create *air patterns*.

In the example given a line similar to a figure S is drawn in the air by the right arm.

The sequence of the motions shows changing weight-levels.

The arm is swinging around the right shoulder as its hub or *centre*, from which all the directions radiate. No steps are made during the arm movement, but as the level is changed, the knees are accordingly bent or stretched. (*See* graph 40.)

Note that in the two final movements the arm will reach behind the back.

43

44. Smooth transitions from one weight-level to another are indicated by *double-shaded* motion characters.

The direction is indicated by the *whole* sign. The level changes during the transference of the weight of the step. The graph shows a sequence of steps in which, during the first step, the knee is first bent and then stretched. In the second step, the level falls from the balls of the feet to the whole foot, but the knee is still stretched. In the next step, the level falls from high to low, the latter involving the bending of the knee, while in the last step the level falls from medium to low.

44

45. A leg gesture with mounting level precedes two steps of different levels.

46. Three steps, each remaining on one level, are accompanied by one slow arm gesture (sideways right), the level of which is changed twice, gradually mounting from low through medium to high. The arm gesture is ended with a quick zigzag of varying "width" in three directions, the middle one of which is an intermediate direction.

45

Note that target points between two neighbouring directions can be indicated by writing the two directions and connecting them with a small vertical simultaneity bow with a dot in it. In this way one can, for instance, express an intermediate direction, say, between forwards and high left forward, etc.

The weight centre of the body, or centre of gravity, above the pelvis region of the trunk, can be raised or lowered by stretching and bending of the supporting limbs.

In sitting and lying this is not the case. The weight centre in these two support situations is invariably on the ground. This position of the weight centre is indeed its medium height, since it can sink still lower till it is *below the support*, for instance, in hanging by the arms (or the feet, etc.) from the branch of a tree or the rung of a ladder. In standing even with bent knees, the weight centre is at a high level, above the ground.

This is important in crouching positions, when the knees are bent much more than in even a low step. In crouching,

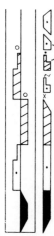

46

The direction signs are now written narrower in relation to the staff columns. In this way there is more room between the signs making the kinetogram more readable. A new rule has also been adopted. The resting of the weight on the supporting leg must each time be confirmed (retention sign).

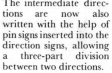

The intermediate directions are now also written with the help of pin signs inserted into the direction signs, allowing a three-part division between two directions.

the weight centre comes "near" to its medium level, as in sitting, without, however, being fully on the ground which supports the body.

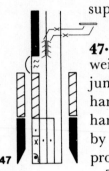

47   **47·** The body is at first in a crouching position, with the weight centre "near" to medium (*i.e.* to sitting). Then a jump occurs, with a transference of the support to both hands gripping the bar. (Objects touched, gripped or handled by a moving person have to be drawn or described by words. There exist no conventional signs for objects or properties used by a dancer on the stage.)

The symbol for the centre of gravity is now ●

The weight centre, having been lifted in the elevation, falls down *below* the support in hanging. In hanging on the arms the weight centre is "very deep."

48. In the transition from one position to the next, a doubt can arise whether a step or an arm gesture has to pass in front of or behind the body.

In such cases, pin-shaped relation signs are used, which do not indicate by themselves any movement, but point to regions of space which are of importance to the movement, *e.g.* above or below, and in front or behind.

48   This graph shows several steps to the right; the left step crosses the first time in front of, and the second time behind the body.

49· Through the pin-shaped relation sign near the motion character in question, it is made clear that the left-arm gesture passes in front of the body, the step and the right-arm gesture pass behind the body.

49

50. *Changes of front* and other rotations are indicated by turning signs:

(*a*) Anti-clockwise (to the left) half-turn. The pin-sign inserted into the turning sign indicates that the new front faces in the direction which was previously backwards.

50   a   b   c d

(*b*) Anti-clockwise (to the left) full turn. The pin-sign indicates that the body pivots until the old "in front" region is re-established.

(*c*) Clockwise (to the right) half-turn.

(*d*) Clockwise (to the right) full turn.

Changes of front or turns of the whole body are inserted in the support column.

Any degree of turn is indicated by a pin-sign. Changes of front of $\frac{1}{8}$, $\frac{1}{4}, \frac{3}{8}, \frac{1}{2}, \frac{5}{8}, \frac{3}{4}, \frac{7}{8}$, and full turns (clockwise or anti-clockwise) can be indicated.

51. Right step forwards, medium; clockwise quarter-turn on right foot; left step forwards, medium (in new front).

After this, a quick right step backwards, deep, followed by a quick anti-clockwise half-turn.

Note: This turn needs a strong impetus of either the upper part of the body or the free-swinging leg; no description for this auxiliary motion is given in this simplified example of notation.

In KIN the weight has to be transferred first before the turn may occur in reality. Therefore the vertical bow connecting the turn sign with a step will not be written. The pin signs now indicate the relationship of one foot to another.

Following this is a left foot step to the right, followed by a slow anti-clockwise $\frac{1}{8}$-turn.

The next movement is a right-foot step to the left connected with an anti-clockwise $\frac{3}{4}$-turn; a left step closes the left foot with the right.

Note that the pin-signs near a step are relation signs, indicating the passing of the step behind the body (*a*) and in front of the body (*b*).

52. If, as in the beginning of this example, one leg maintains some support, the weight will remain on both legs. In this graph a half-turn on both legs brings the left leg into a backwards position, while the right leg comes in front.

Right and left steps are made, forwards, on the balls of the feet. The weight is carried by both legs. A half-turn to the right results in the right leg now standing forwards, in relation to the new front, both legs at deep level. Both arms are raised during the turn.

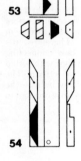

53. A turning jump. The right leg steps to the right. After a clockwise jumping half-turn in the air, the left foot takes over the weight a step-length to the left and completes the clockwise half-turn to a full turn.

With a stand on the right foot with bent knees, the original front is reached again in a starting position, from which the same turning jump could be repeated, but this time anti-clockwise to the left, starting with a left step.

54. *Rotations* (clockwise or anti-clockwise) of arms and legs are indicated by the turn-signs inserted in the corresponding columns.

Now white pin signs are used in the turn signs indicating out- and in-turn in relation to the body.

Black pin signs indicate out- or in-turn in relation to the last achieved position.

$\frac{1}{8}$ to left $\frac{1}{8}$ to right

The pin sign inserted into the path sign now indicates the degree of circling in a similar way to turn signs. (In this case it is $\frac{1}{4}$ circular path, clockwise.) The new front is now indicated with an auxiliary sign written outside the kinetogram.

55. *Circular or curved path* signs refer to a series of steps which describe a circle or a part of it. Graph 55 shows five steps forward on a path representing a quarter of a circle. (To complete the whole circle would take twenty steps, each five steps resulting in a quarter circle.) The path in this example is curved. In the gap in the path-sign the final new front is inserted, which indicates subdivisions of the circle. The front of the body is continuously changing as it goes along the circular pathway.

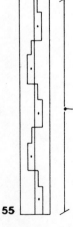

56. *Anti-clockwise circular path* (half-circle) with right sideways steps.

(Note: When stepping anti-clockwise to the right, the moving person is compelled in this example to stand and progress with his front facing towards the centre of the circular path.)

In KIN the anti-clockwise circular path sign is written on the left side of the stave. The clockwise circular path is written on the right side of the stave. In LAB all are written on the right side of the stave.

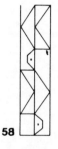

57. *Direct* or straight path-signs have in some cases to be written, *e.g.* in hopping on both feet, if a slight progression in a definite direction is made by this means.

Now the following sign is used

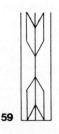

58. The rotation of the whole body in a *cartwheel* is notated with the help of a variant of the turn sign. In this graph a cartwheel to the right is followed by a cartwheel to the left.

The cartwheel sign is now written

cartwheel to the right

cartwheel to the left

59. Other variants of rotations are the *somersault*, forwards and backwards.

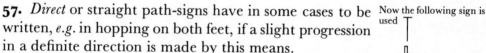

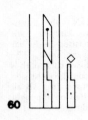

60. The small diamond-shaped space-holding sign after a gesture means that the part of the body thus designated remains in the same position in space while other parts are turning in different directions.

In this example, without the space-holding sign the forward-stretched right arm would follow the turn and would point "forwards" in relation to the new front. *With the space-holding sign* the arm remains where it is in space, and therefore points "backwards" at the end of the turn.

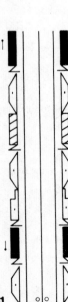

61. Some of the intermediate space-directions or deviations of movement-targets (*see* graph 46) are of particular importance owing to the symmetrical structure of the body. All directions originate from or are related to a hub (*see* explanations to graph 41).

The arms are frequently moved in directions which are related to the centre or to the central plane dividing the left and right sides of the body. This applies to all forwards and backwards directions of the trunk and also to its normal, vertical, low and high positions.

There are several ways of writing these directions for arm movements, in fixing definite arm positions similar to the dance positions of the feet. In movement notation I prefer a small angular bracket connecting the arm column with the trunk column. This bracket indicates that the arms have to be directed into the corresponding trunk directions. In graph 61, such deviations of the target are shown: in the directions deep, forwards and high above the head. The deep signs show the deep low positions in front of and behind the trunk. Backward targets can be deviated in the same way.

The angular bracket is no longer used.

62. This graph shows *diversions* or deflections of the movement path. The diversion signs are very small directional signs (mostly diagonals) which indicate in the example, for instance, that the first arm movement does not proceed directly from left diagonal backwards to high right, but that the movement takes a roundabout path through diagonal left high forwards. Such a diversion passes the indicated direction by deflecting slightly towards it, without really reaching it.

Many deflecting movements of this kind can be followed between two points of space.

The other two diversions lead:

(for the left arm) through diagonal right deep forwards to left deep;

(for the second movement of the right arm) through diagonal right high backwards to diagonal right forwards.

At the end there is a deviation of the high direction of both arms into a high position directly over the head, finishing in an ordinary sideways gesture for both arms.

The diversion sign indicated is no longer used. Deviations (detours) are now written with the pin sign written into the vertical bow.

63–68. Amongst the significant changes of position in space, those in which opposite directions are combined into one motif play a dominant rôle.

It is important for the notator, and simplifies his task, if he can easily recognise and discern such changes.

It is possible to distinguish regions of space which are most easily reached by one of the arms or a leg, while movements into opposite directions or regions often involve a certain contortion and strain. The simple notation of opposite directions can, in some cases of harmonious movement, replace the detailed description of the various bendings and stretchings, shiftings and tiltings, turns, twists and rotations, described by pin-signs, which are involved in the more contorted parts of a motif.

Six examples of motifs containing changes in opposite directions are shown in the graphs 63–68. It can easily be imagined that in a manner not unlike that seen in the time rhythm, which is built up from contrasting quick

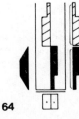

and slow movement durations, a space-rhythm or harmony can be discerned, consisting in principle of the alterations of contrasting movement directions. The contrasts shown here are:

65

63. high right *v.* deep left

66

64. deep backwards *v.* high forwards

65. left forwards *v.* right backwards

67

66. deep right *v.* high left

67. high backwards *v.* deep forwards

68

68. right forwards *v.* left backwards.

Note: The participation of the trunk in an arm move-ment is indicated in notation by an angular bow in the trunk column. See this bow in the six motifs in the graphs 63–68.

This symbol is called the inclusion bow. [

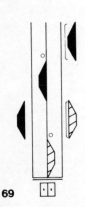

69

69. In this graph the end position of motif 63 is not reached in one simultaneous movement, but is successively de-veloped.

70. The same is the case in graph 70. The end position of motif 66 is reached here, but by successive development rather than by simultaneous movement.

Note: It is perhaps interesting for the notator to become conscious of the similarity between body positions and chords in music, while the successive development of the final position is more akin to the progression of melody in music.

The contortion and strain in one part of a motif calls for the release of such tension, which release is similar to progression or resolution in harmony, *i.e.* the re-establishment of a natural balance.

The recognition of such transitions from spatial strain to release is of great value in the observation and description of movement.

71. The face—signalised by a head sign in an oval frame —is oriented in space by "looking" into a definite direction.

In this graph the face "looks" into four different directions, which could not be expressed by notating all the tiltings and turnings of the head involved in this movement —some notators use a square frame around the head sign.

All notators now use a square frame with a stroke indicating the frontal surface of the head = face.

72. It is also possible to consider other parts of the body, such as the palms of the hands (or even the soles of the feet) as facing in some direction or, as it were, "looking" somewhere. Graph 72 shows the palms of both hands as first facing each other and then "looking" together, downwards and forwards, with a smooth transition through medium forwards to high forwards.

The palm is now written

Note: Palm "facings" should not involve arm movements if these are not especially prescribed.

The chest is also a part of the body which can be often advantageously described as facing a direction, instead of tilting towards it. In this case the chest sign has to be put into a square or oval frame.

All notators now also use square frames for the chest sign

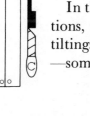

SECTION C

The notation of the stresses of movement

As has been seen before, in movement notation the accentuation of the first movement in regular beats can be expressed by inserting bar lines, as in music.

Apart from this, the particular stress laid on a part of a motif is indicated in movement notation by an accent comma which is used in two shades:

A black comma for particularly "strong" movements.

A white comma for particularly "light" movements.

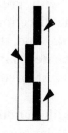

73. This graph shows three low stamping steps on "place" (*see* explanation to graphs 40 and 41) which will produce a more or less audible sound or noise.

73

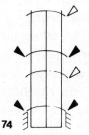

74. Stressed arm or hand movement can also produce a sound. In this graph a clapping of hands is notated. In the first and third strong claps, both hands are *hit* together. In the second and fourth light claps, the high hand alone hits the immobile left hand.

Note: the distances between the hits indicate different durations, so that a definite rhythm comes about.

74

75. A stressed arm movement in the air in which no sound is produced. This graph records a "punch"-like *thrust* in which both arms stretch in a direct line diagonally upwards.

75

43

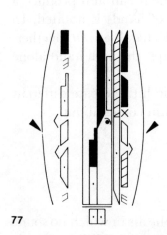

76. This graph shows a hopping on the left foot, tapping or *dabbing* at the same time lightly with the toes of the right foot on the ground. The taps are made, first in front; second, on the right side; and, third, behind. In the last hop both feet join together on "place." A hook connecting a leg gesture with the support column indicates that the foot touches the floor. Such floor touch signs pointing forwards mean touching with the toes, pointing backwards with the heel, pointing forwards and backwards with the whole foot.

77. All the movements of this motif are strongly stressed, *i.e.* performed with great muscular energy. As a result of the directions of the steps and trunk movements, and the simultaneous rotations of the indicated parts of the arms, a "wringing"-like twist of the whole body takes place.

Note that in the graphs 73–77 bodily actions, such as "stamping," "hitting," "clapping," "tapping," "dabbing," "punch-like thrusting" and "wringing" have occurred.

In the notation of everyday movements, *e.g.* some of the actions occurring in industrial operations, or in dramatic performances, it is sometimes possible to dispense with the detailed description of the shapes and rhythms and to record more briefly only the action character of the movement.

For industrial purposes a more elaborate notation of the details of stresses is normally used. This is described in my book *Effort* (Macdonald & Evans Ltd., London).

To the central diagonal stroke of the "effort" signs, which represents the "accent," small affixes are added, indicating special qualities of the accent.

As it is sometimes useful to notate subtleties of accent-combinations also in recording dances, abbreviated signs have therefore been introduced which are shown together with the original industrial signs in the graphs 78, 79, 80, 81.

These are adjustments of the standard effort signs to be used in conjunction with movement notation.

In the left vertical columns (*a, b, c, d*) some fundamental industrial effort signs are represented, while in the right vertical columns (*a₁, b₁, c₁, d₁*) the corresponding abbreviations used in dance notation are shown.

Note: The key to the abbreviation signs is:

(1) If the main diagonal stroke of the accent sign is inclined to the right the stress is "direct."

(2) If the main diagonal stroke is inclined to the left the stress is "flexible" (roundabout).

(3) A single diagonal stroke indicates a "light" stress.

(4) A double diagonal stroke indicates a "strong" stress.

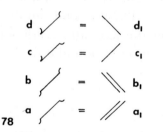

78. 78*a* and *a₁* indicate a strong and direct stress.

78*b* and *b₁* indicate a strong and flexible stress.

78*c* and *c₁* indicate a light and direct stress.

78*d* and *d₁* indicate a light and flexible stress.

The graphs shown in 79 are the same as in 78 with a small horizonal stroke added at the left side, which stroke is the sign of sustainment. With this addition a series of basic actions can be characterised.

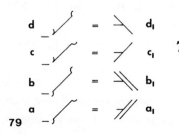

79. 79*a* and *a₁* indicate "pressing," which is strong, direct and sustained.

79*b* and *b₁* indicate "wringing," which is strong, flexible and sustained.

79*c* and *c₁* indicate "gliding," which is

light, direct and sustained.

79d and d_1 indicate "floating," which is light, flexible and sustained.

The graphs shown in 80 are again the same as in 78, but the small horizontal stroke is added at the right side, which stroke is the sign of quickness. With this addition another series of basic actions are characterised.

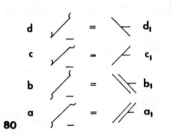

80. 80a and a_1 indicate "punching," which is strong, direct and quick.

80b and b_1 indicate "slashing," which is strong, flexible and quick.

80c and c_1 indicate "dabbing," which is light, direct and quick.

80d and d_1 indicate "flicking," which is light, flexible and quick.

The graphs shown in 81 have as an affix to the four fundamental forms of 78 a slightly longer horizontal stroke. This stroke is immediately connected with the lower end of the main diagonal and signifies the "flow" of the stress. This affix written on the left side stands for "free flow." Written on the right side the affix signifies "bound flow."

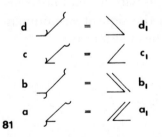

81. 81a and a_1 indicate a stress which is strong, direct and bound.

81b and b_1 indicate a stress which is strong, flexible and free.

81c and c_1 indicate a stress which is light, direct and bound.

81d and d_1 indicate a stress which is light, flexible and free.

Note: An additional flow indication of either kind—free or bound—can be added to any other simple or combined stress.

Accent or stress signs in dance notation are not intended to replace the exact description of body parts, rhythm, and patterns. They can, however, express briefly the whole action-character of an elaborate motif. Thus, for instance, the whole character of graph 77 could be summarised by the stress sign for "wringing," which would enable the reader to realise this character at one glance.

The stress and action factors of Section C are of great interest in the study of the psychological implications of movement.

SECTION D

Some examples of the practical application of the script

82–86. *A series of 5 fundamental jumps*

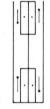

82. A jump from both feet, ending with both feet on the same spot, but changing the position of the feet from right foot in front to left foot in front (*"changement"*).

82

Note: the pin-shaped signs show the relative position of the feet. The jump is indicated by the gap between the two steps. The gap shows that the body has no support, and therefore must, for a moment, hover in the air. The time in the air is determined by the length of the gap.

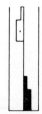

83

83. A jump from both feet ending on one foot, travelling forwards (*"sissonne"* form).

84

84. A hop from one foot on to the same foot, travelling forwards (*"temps levé"* form).

85

85. Leaping forwards from the right to the left foot (*"jeté"* form).

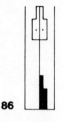

86. A jump from one foot on to both feet, travelling forwards (*"assemblé"* form).

87 **86.**

87–91. *The five basic foot positions.*

87. First position; the feet are together side by side.

88. Second position: the feet are set apart sideways, usually with a foot-length distance between them.

89. Third position: the feet are together, the right foot half way across in front of the left.

Note: the left foot can similarly be in front of the right, in which case the pin-signs will have to be altered accordingly.

90. Fourth position: the feet are set apart in a forward-backward position, usually with a foot-length distance between them.

In open positions, a step-length's distance between the feet is understood.

91. Fifth position: the feet are together, the right foot fully across in front of the left, so that its heel touches the toes of the latter. The note to graph 89 also applies here.

Note: The 180° out-turn of classical ballet has to be indicated by turn and rotation signs in the leg gesture column. In- and out-turns used in special dance styles are not included in the basic movement positions.

92–97. *Further details of positions, jumps, etc.*

92. A fourth position, right foot in front, in which the feet stand in exactly the same relationship as in the fifth position, namely across one another, but are separated by the length of a foot.

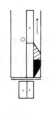

93. The left foot supports part of the weight throughout, while the stepping leg goes from first position to fourth in front, and to second and to fourth behind.

Now two retention signs are necessary, (*see* graph 45).

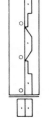

94. The right leg closes behind the left foot in fifth position after a high gesture to the right (*"grand battement"* form).

95. Open (second) position; the right foot closes up to the left, taking over the whole weight. The square vertical bracket links the right step to the left foot, indicating that the right foot goes beside the spot where the left was.

In LAB this sign is called the "staple." In KIN it may be written, but generally there is no need for it.

96. Swaying the weight of the body from second position over to the right and then to the left foot. The sideways steps go to the same spots where the feet were in the second position.

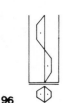

97. Hopping to the left on the right foot. At the start, the left leg is already lifted, so that when the standing leg comes off the floor a jump is made.

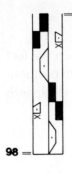

98–100. *Three simple National Dance steps.*

98. A Tarantella step; during the hop the free leg is lifted bent across the other side. Notice the repetition signs, used also in 99 and 100.

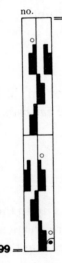

99. A Czardas step: the movement is performed without rise and fall. During the low steps forward, the level of the centre of gravity remains strictly the same. This is indicated by the "hold" after the pelvis sign.

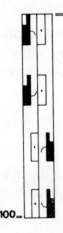

100. A typical dance step, hopping and touching the floor first with the toe and then the heel.

101–108. *Examples of various motifs displaying agility.*

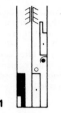

101. Falling forward on to both hands.

Note: falling or loss of balance results when the centre of gravity is for a moment not above the feet, *i.e.* not in a vertical line with the support.

101

102. "Arabesque"-like position, the body being supported by the right knee and hand.

102

103. The basic movement directions of a typical classical ballet "attitude."

103

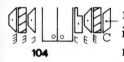

104. A stylised angular position, such as might appear in oriental dances or frescoes of ancient Egyptian movement. The position is a complex one, and the graph is inevitably complex also.

104

Note: Remember that when the elbow sign is written, it is the upper arm that moves in the direction stated; when the wrist sign is written, it is the lower arm that moves. The same applies for the various parts of the leg: when the knee sign is written, it is the thigh that moves so that the knee points into the direction stated; when the ankle sign is written, it is the lower part of the leg that moves.

105. A dance step sequence in which the motif of sliding the feet over the floor alternates with leg gestures, the legs being lifted from the floor.

Starting position: legs astride, medium level stance. Without elevating them into the air (since there are no jumping gaps) slide the feet together into first position

105

medium level, then apart into fourth position high level, right foot front. After a pause for one beat the weight is lowered on the right foot and the left lifted off the ground behind. Notice the angular vertical bracket in the right leg column which shows that "place" (*see* explanation to graphs 40 and 41) is the spot where the right foot stood previously, although the weight is shifted forward when the left foot is released.

The movement on beat 4 may also be written without the bracket (staple, *see* graph 34), but an indication of direction is needed. (The centre of gravity moves forward in this example.)

Now the tip of the left foot slides through the first position (two floor touch signs connected with one gesture means sliding) and the weight is transferred left sideways on to the left leg. The right foot performs a short touch of the floor before stepping out to the right, while the left leg retains weight, thus ending in a second position.

Whilst the one leg is gesturing the other one has to take the weight. For this reason a retention sign is needed on beats 5 and 7, (*see* graph 17).

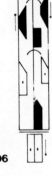

106. The legs beat together in the air (*"cabriole," "assemblé battu"*).

107. Lying on the back, supported on seat (two hip signs) and shoulders.

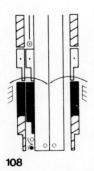

108. Bending backwards to touch the floor with the hands (bridge), and coming up again. For the return to the upright the usual directional sign "high" may be used in the trunk column. Here a special "return to normal" sign (last sign in the left trunk column) is shown.

One now uses [symbol] to indicate the trunk.

Note: This sign (circle with a dot) is used for any part of the body when it returns to its normal carriage from a special position. The duration line after the sign indicates the relative length of the time used for this return.

This is still used in LAB. KIN uses ∧

as the general "back-to-normal" sign.

109–114. *Examples of partners moving together.*

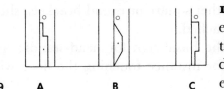

109   A   B   C

109. Three people move together, each stepping in a different direction. If several people move in a different manner at the same time, each is given an individual staff which is joined by a straight line to the others, thus forming a group score.

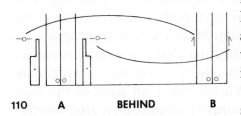

110   A   BEHIND   B

110. Two people standing together. Partner A stretches his arms forward and touches B's shoulders. The signs with two ends with white centres, indicate that A touches B's shoulders "from above," right hand on right shoulder, left hand on left shoulder.

Note: If no particular part of the limbs is mentioned, it is the end which touches, *i.e.* hands or feet.

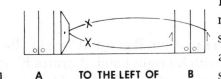

111   A   TO THE LEFT OF   B

111. A holds B with his right arm round both shoulders. The narrow sign in the bracket means that the arm is bent and *embraces* the partner's shoulders. It is written near the active part, which is in this case A's right arm.

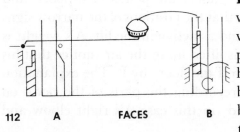

112   A   FACES   B

112. A holds a basket high and forwards, carrying it from underneath with his flat left hand without gripping with his fingers. B stands on his head and touches the basket from behind with his left foot. The angular brackets (in A's staff) indicate that the weight of an object or person is carried, as opposed to the curved brackets (in **B**'s staff) (touch signs) showing that no weight is taken. B also touches the floor with his hands. The pin signs, in connection with either square or round brackets, show from which side the object is approached.

B's head-stand is recorded by the basic sign for head-stands; any further details of the position, as for instance touching the floor with both hands, must be added.

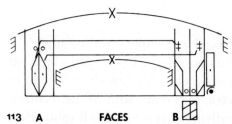

113   A   FACES   B

113. Standing on a partner's knees. A's weight is carried on B's knees, B crouching down with legs out-turned. Both hold hands. Notice the angular brackets without grasp, indicating that the weight is carried by letting it rest on the supporting parts of the body (in this case B's knees). Since all parts of the body carrying its weight are written in the support column, no matter whether the weight is carried by the floor, or by objects, or by other persons, A's position with legs astride, on B's knees is shown in the support column. The narrow sign in the centre of the curved ("touch") brackets indicates that both partners grip the hands of the other in the touch.

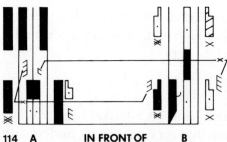

114   A   IN FRONT OF   B

114. A lift. B grasps A's right elbow with his right hand. A grasps B's left wrist with his left hand. The angular brackets with the narrow sign indicate carrying with hand grasp. Notice also that the angular brackets connect the points of support, and that the positions of the narrow signs show A's left hand and B's right hand as active in the lift. A's weight is supported by these two grasps and is lifted up in the air (notice that his two legs are shown as being finally off the floor) by B. The explanation of graph 33 shows the method of recording the parts of the body on which the body weight is supported (in this case A's right elbow and left hand).

Note on Staging Signs.

The place of a person on a definite spot in space, say, on the stage, can be inserted in the form of a floor design and made more precise by additional notes in words. The same is the case with positions in relation to a partner or a group. (*See* graphs 110–114, where it is indicated by words whether the person A stands behind the person B, or facing B, or in front of B.)

New symbols for all these circumstances are used. Area signs indicate the area, *e.g.* the central area of the floor ◧ the forward central area of the floor, etc. ⬓

Special group movement signs belong to the category of staging signs. The ingenious system of group movement symbols, which has been developed by Professor A. Knust, can be highly recommended. The details of staging signs fall however outside this introduction into the principles of body movement notation.

Relationship signs indicate the relation of the partners to each other, etc. *e.g.* the boy is standing behind the girl ⬍ the girl is standing in front of the boy. each boy has one girl on his right each girl has one boy on her left

INDEX A

List of Signs in Alphabetical Order

INDEX B

List of Movements in the Order of Graph Numbers